David's
of book
Nonsense

David . S . Willcocks

Graphic design by : - Fox Graphics

First published in 2013 by Cathkin Peak Publishing.

First printed in 2013 by Crewe Colour Printers Ltd.

www.davidsbookofnonsense.com

Acknowledgements

To my wife Ann, for her patience and advice.
To my family, and to those friends and colleagues who believed
in the concept for this book right from the very start and who
supported me throughout. Thank you.

Special thanks also to Pat Hobel in South Africa
for his excellent sketches.

To Lyndon Murgatroyd, local Cheshire Historian and writer, and
to John Lindley, local poet and writer, for their valuable advice and
assistance despite which, I still went ahead with this book.

paperback

ISBN 978-0-9576310-0-7

Contents

Contents

David's *of* *book* **Nonsense**

Foreword

Being attracted to windswept and interesting people, it was hardly surprising that I sparked up a conversation with David. He has that look that says "Try me, I've got things to say".

I was indeed as invariably happens, bang on with my assumption. David is a very amusing man, his ability to play the English language makes for a truly refreshing little book that will bring a smirk to the grumpiest face. I am a writer and comedian myself, in fact we met on board a cruise ship where I was plying my trade and I hope to know David for a good time yet.

He explained to me his idea for a book which I believe you will agree, has been executed magnificently. As with most "ideas for books" it was destined to remain just that so I am glad I had a hand in making the idea a reality. Do it or else, I think was the persuasive term I used, and so here it is.

It is a book for everywhere, anytime, any mood. Just dip in when you fancy for an instant fix to cure the absurdities of life, pick a line to set you up for the working day, or relax you for the evening. Pretentious it ain't, funny it is, it's probably very clever too, but I fear that admission may swell the author's head. As for me? I'm pretty proud of myself, what a wonderful choice of person to chat to I made!

Kevin McCarthy
Kevin is "Man with the beard" from The Comedy Club Ltd, Stand up comedy, Master of Ceremonies, Television appearances, Writer and many other virtues...
See him on Youtube.

Introduction

The English language is a clever old girl, she has so many twists & turns with sometimes double, indeed treble or more meanings for the same word, albeit different spellings. It lends itself to puns.

So, why this book of nonsense ? Well, it started in the year 2000, I was in a bar in a State (no, not "in a state", but "in a State !") ... see, you're on the same wavelength already. The State in question was Massachusetts USA and behind the bar was a sign inviting one to ponder - "What did we go back to before the drawing board ?" What indeed ... It rather got me thinking and upon returning to the UK started to compile my own one-line-trivia philosophic nonsense sayings. It just seemed to escalate from there.

Anyway, enjoy the concept. It's aimed to bring a smile (or a groan) to all ages and to be enjoyed whilst commuting on the bus or train, at the airport or on the plane, on the cruise ship, by the pool, on the beach, in the garden, in waiting rooms, at break times, in the coffee shop, in the bath (waterproof edition available soon), in your favourite armchair or in bed ... anywhere you choose !

Either way, dear reader, please enjoy these nonsensical sayings, escape our sometimes troubled world and step into the slightly ridiculous one that our language provides for us. After all, "it is a punny old world".
ps: This book comes with a warning ... there may be a follow up !

David . S . Willcocks
Cheshire, England.

David's *book* *of* *Nonsense*

On Manufacturing & Industry

early attempts to make aluminium paper were often foiled.

*those employed in soft drinks firms always
enjoy a cordial atmosphere.*

never ask an elevator salesman for a lift.

*incompetent human cannonballs are obviously
not the right calibre of person.*

hard working mechanics sometimes need a brake.

women who join the perfume industry know it makes scents.

changing your hairdresser can mean a sorrowful parting.

furniture restorers sometimes varnish into thin air.

a good tea lady really urns her wages.

On Manufacturing & Industry

do washroom attendants get a day in loo ?

being a milkman is not for everyone and some bottle out.

tunnel contractors sometimes find their work boring.

fed up builders often throw the trowel in.

errant archaeologists ruin their chances.

blacksmiths often like to forge a relationship.

cutlery salesmen have a tendency to be blunt.

don't get fobbed off with poor quality key rings.

Tailoring, Textiles & Clothing

a good seamstress is hard to pin down.

textile workers don't pass away, they simply dye.

employees in Lycra factories tend to work long stretches.

bossy supervisors in clothing factories can be right
sew and sews.

recently, sales of hats and caps have reached their peak.

manufacturers of men's singlets may have
a vested interest.

manufacturers of facecloths may give you
a load of flannel.

shoe repairer conventions are just a lot of cobblers.

Tailoring, Textiles & Clothing

an expensive set of hankies is not to be sneezed at.

tailors sometimes leave under their own free twill.

to wear one glove is sensible, but on the other hand ...

quilts are not a patch on what they used to be.

unscrupulous tailors will try and stitch you up.

textile workers are generally a close knit team.

when garment menders get cross, tempers get frayed.

after an argument, tailors tend to patch things up.

The Economy

recently, many tiling centres have closed and gone to the wall.

*beach ball sales are currently down, but they'll
soon bounce back.*

despite the recession, car makers have had a bumper year.

in these difficult times even tea drinkers are feeling the strain.

in the recession, some fish restaurants have taken a battering.

the price of fireworks seems to rocket every year.

not everyone has cottoned on to the recent rise in textiles.

the cost of hot air balloon flights is soaring.

The Economy

in this recession, blacksmiths have taken quite a hammering.

in the recession, even accordion clubs have felt the squeeze.

in this recession, even 100 pence has taken a pounding.

the cost of bell tower steps is spiralling.

in this recession even boiled egg and soldiers have taken a dip.

*in this recession several watch companies have been
wound up.*

*when string manufacturers have to close, it's not for
the sake of twine.*

the ongoing recession means our origami club has folded.

the price of washing lines has recently been pegged.

The Economy

the price of fridges has been frozen for the third year running.

tax inspectors live off the VAT of the land.

those who invest in coal often take a lump sum.

in a recession, potato growers are quick to chip in.

the recent price rise of potato crisps will cost us all a packet.

in this recession even steam boiler makers are under pressure.

recently there has been a serge in the price of textiles.

dentists are bracing themselves for another recession.

Hobbies

since our local scrabble club closed, we are lost for words.

cheat at dominoes and you will be spotted.

a heavy picnic basket will hamper your enjoyment.

*when travelling together to the swimming baths,
use the pool car.*

our woodwork class has split and formed a splinter group.

too many nights under canvas can lead to a tents situation.

there is always a long cue outside popular snooker clubs.

if offered a trampoline, one must jump at the chance.

Hobbies

karate is enjoyable and people get a kick out of it.

jogging is beneficial in the long run.

the cost of owning a glider is soaring.

the art of magic is fast disappearing.

hiking clubs attract people from all walks of life.

some board games look a bit dicey to me.

*the best campsites in England are found
near Stoke-on-Tent.*

speakers at hiking club meetings tend to ramble on a bit.

books about pliers are not exactly gripping reading.

Campanology

some Campanologists are well past their bell by date.

recently, the art of bell ringing has lost it's a- peal.

never ask a campanologist to give you a bell.

campanologists caught in a rainstorm will be ringing wet.

The Weather

climate experts sometimes feel under the weather.

meteorologists work better under high pressure.

dismissed weather presenters sometimes leave
under a cloud.

weatthr, wheatre, wehetre, wetrrhe; that was
a terrible spell of weather.

On Sport

guilty wicket keepers are often released on bail.

football teams playing on stony pitches usually
win on aggregate.

too much jogging is sole destroying.

i'm not keen on ice skating, it leaves me cold.

when you are ill, your motor sport friends will rally round.

the sale of bogus tennis equipment is simply a racket.

in football play down the wing, in an aircraft, don't.

to become a top sports coach you'll need 52 seats
and a driver.

never ask a tennis player to serve lunch.

David's book of Nonsense

Cooking, Catering, Food & Drink

cheese is so annoying, it really grates.

to make ketchup you must have the necessary re-sauces.

insist on the best kitchen utensils and go for designer ladles.

never drink alcohol from a shoe, it might be laced.

boxes of corn flakes should always carry a cereal number.

"pi r squared" is not true because pies tend to be round.

emotional things wedding cakes, always in tiers.

when buying a brewery, the VAT is usually included.

before making scrambled eggs, do a whisk assessment.

David's
of book
Nonsense

Cooking, Catering, Food & Drink

some distillery workers simply gin and bear it.

when picnicking in Cheddar, don't gorge yourself.

incompetent chefs will get a roasting from their boss.

when large fruit is sad, it becomes meloncholy.

the tastiest broth is found in a soupermarket.

peaches can be really irritating and give you the pip.

using the same teabag for 7 days will make week tea.

brewers stay on to the bitter end.

there's no fast way to make sloe gin.

Chefs & Butchers

chefs will make half-baked excuses about undercooked food.

chefs marry for batter of worse.

some chefs are bad drivers and will carve you up.

do Japanese butchers still sell karate chops ?

straight talking butchers never mince their words.

never bet with your butcher, there is too much at steak.

some chefs drive souped up cars.

when butchers shops close, staff get the chop.

David's book of Nonsense

About Bakers

bread makers look to the yeast for inspiration.

bread making is popular and is on the rise.

bakers shops usually have a morning roll call.

to the French, baking bread is a pain.

before you bake a loaf of bread, buy everything you knead.

why do we have a "round of sandwiches" when bread is square?

one cannot find good baking flour for loaf nor money.

the annual baker's awards always finish with a toast.

The Alphabet & Grammar

leave extra time for the alphabet, you may need a P.

leave extra time for the alphabet, there may be a Q.

who invented the alphabet and Y?

be polite to the alphabet and mind your P's and Q's.

*beware when using hyphen's, you don't want your
your hopes dashed.*

*some people remove letters from the alphabet and
become B keepers.*

the alphabet often does things in X S.

when mariners go from A to B they tend to go by C.

David's
book
of Nonsense

All about Appearances

hairdressing is a costly profession with many overheads.

some people have hair to dye for.

when women go to the hairdresser they expect mirror-curls.

women can get quite scentimental about perfumes.

when buying a wig, it's case of toupee or not toupee.

those who buy an expensive woollen jumper have been fleeced.

outside men's hairdresser's there is often a barber-queue.

the use of botox is frowned upon by many.

many a diet falls by the weighside.

David's
of book
Nonsense

It's a Dog's Life

*although nice animals, boxer dogs are pretty useless
in the ring.*

beware when buying a gundog, they rarely shoot anything.

stubborn kennel owners can be rather dogmatic.

dalmatian dogs are easy to spot.

buying a dog will give you a new leash of life.

letting sleeping dogs lie means we'll never get the truth.

a dog with a hangover will feel wruff.

with some dogs it's a case of buy one, get one flea.

Cats & Rabbits

Cats

to stop the cat from scratching the dvd, press the paws button.

if the cat eats your trainers, shoe it out.

felines find their way with cat nav.

cats always seem to get the fastest lap.

not all cats are purrfect.

Rabbits

some rabbits book hare appointments.

some rabbits are comedians and think they are bunny.

David's
book
of Nonsense

Horses, Sheep & Cattle

Horses

old racehorses do tend to nag a bit.

shouting too loudly at the races will make you horse.

difficulty in selling your horse may leave you saddled with it.

Sheep

sheep farming is shear delight.

indecisive sheep will make a ewe turn.

Cattle

cattle are often seen and herd.

upset a cow and it will be in a bad mooood.

some cattle are brave and some cow-herds.

sheep often communicate with baaa coding.

Pigs

a pig with laryngitis soon becomes disgruntled.

pigs do tend to hog the limelight.

keeping a pig clean is a swine of a job.

if fibs are porkies, what do pigs call them ?

we make a "pigs ear" out of something, so what do pigs call it ?

the best bacon comes from Porktugal.

every morning pigs face the daily rind.

a hamlet is not a small pig !

General Animals & Insects

those who pay to see buffalo can expect a hefty charge.

healthy porcupines are evidence that acupuncture works.

animals always have a tail to tell.

*some large apes have a sweet tooth, especially
the meringue-utan.*

hyenas are no laughing matter.

some elks are sent on a wild moose chase.

the new animal welfare group is called "help the paw".

many antelopes carry a mobile fawn.

David's
of book
Nonsense

Birdlife

many caged songbirds are sold on hire perches.

wading birds learn from experience and once bittern twice shy.

owning a seabird is getting expensive; have you seen the price of petrel?

how migrating birds know their way is anyone's geese.

to arctic seabirds one good tern deserves another.

when speckled birds sing in your garden, it's the thrush hour.

birds of prey like to receive gift vultures.

birds look forward to their sunday roost.

hens laying inferior eggs will make poultry excuses.

Rodents, Reptiles & Amphibians

an angry toad will be hopping mad.

even rodents need a new pair of shrews sometimes.

rodents tend to be very good at mouse-keeping.

a snake on your car bonnet could be a vindscreen viper.

tortoises like to use shell garages.

water voles are always going to the bank.

never ask a crocodile to snap out of it.

being a snail is very expensive, always shelling out.

Transport

putting petrol in a diesel car is rather fuelish.

cyclists without audible means of approach often win the no-bell prize.

chiropodists whose cars break down will always appreciate a toe.

have you ever seen a car boot for sale at a car boot sale?

washing your car with a sponge may leave jam and icing all over it.

mending your bicycle gears is sprocket science.

cycling clubs always need a good spokesman.

eating toast and preservatives in your car may cause traffic jams.

David's
of *book*
Nonsense

Travel

for those who enjoy a large port after dinner, try Rotterdam.

when considering moving to a Scottish Isle, Mull over it first.

when travelling in Wales, one might stop for a leek.

the best accommodation in Egypt is Bedouin & Breakfast.

route finding in some Northern English cities ties you in Notts.

drivers using the Midlands Expressway cannot say they haven't been tolled.

to swim west from Lands End is Scilly.

visitors to the Amazon basin should clean it before they leave.

when lost in the Arctic, go with the floe.

David's ***book*** *of* **Nonsense**

Around the UK & Ireland

people in Lincolnshire think the wold of each other.

people in Chester really do like to be beside the Deeside.

the best place to lose weight in Ireland is Slimerick.

many people in the Scottish Isles receive Skye television.

many firms in Scotland are doing a Stirling job.

we all know the Forth bridge, but where are the other three?

the Scots often see aye to aye.

drivers on the Isle of Wight tend to use the park and Ryde.

On Crime

*bank robbers always get the blame even when
it's not their vault.*

pilfer from the library and they'll throw the book at you.

police cannot find any pattern to the recent spate of quilt thefts.

if your turf is stolen, you will look for-lawn.

remove a large statue in New York and you are taking Liberties.

those caught pilfering fireworks may be let off.

he who trespasses at Wimbledon shall get court.

using lower case letters instead of big letters is a capital offence.

*David's
book
of Nonsense*

On Crime

*following the recent spate of chain fence theft, police think
there is a link.*

*following the spate of wig thefts, police are now
combing the area.*

*confectionery sold in prisons is commonly known
as jailhouse rock.*

they who desecrate statues are making a monumental mistake.

the authorities have issued a stark warning to streakers.

pilfer a calendar and you'll get 12 months.

he accused of verbosity will receive a long sentence.

prisoners should not be released before their cell by date.

Our Relationships

where there's a will, there is a queue of relatives.

friendly things balloons, always popping round.

poets often marry for better or verse.

we remember our first date but what about our first fig.

older people tend to make bus passes at each other.

meeting an old flame can result in a heated discussion.

many brides go to the altar, and some alter afterwards.

some relatives are niece and some are not so niece.

David's
of *book*
Nonsense

Events & the Arts

weird things jumble sales, quite bazaar.

even curtain exhibitions eventually draw to a close.

the annual potato growers convention is always
held in Mashville.

the annual baker's convention always finishes on a roll.

plans for hosting a hand-washing contest have been scrubbed.

when painters receive poor reviews, it can leave
them broken-arted.

roofing conventions always end with night on the tiles.

film makers often do it for reel.

only fair haired actors get to play Jayne's Blonde.

Sea, Coastal & Waterways

distressed seaweed can always ring the kelpline.

the coral seas were discovered by the Irish explorer,
Great Barry O' Reef.

irate sea captains can harbour a grudge.

lighthouse keepers always enjoy a beacon sandwich.

in Scotland, expensive yachts are kept under loch and quay.

in nautical terms, buoys will be buoys.

some narrow boat owners are inconsiderate
and tend to barge in.

life rafts carry flares in case they come back into fashion.

Trees

renovated pine forests always look spruced up.

an annoying tree will very soon become un-poplar.

to age a palm tree, just read the dates on it.

trees come in various sizes, little and larch.

some hedges tend to lead privet lives.

some trees get lonely and pine for each other.

some trees are attractive whilst others are just plane.

using a computer is easy for lumberjacks, they just log on.

Around the Home

when buying settees and chairs, don't accept
suites from strangers.

a new fireplace is a grate idea.

those who cannot afford a new fireplace should not lose hearth.

those who cannot afford a new bookcase should shelve the idea.

if there's a tap on the door, that will be the plumber.

for those buying an apartment, well that's another storey.

good quality oil squeaks for itself.

the price of guttering seems to be going through the roof.

In the Garden

gardeners buried in their allotments should be allowed
to rest in peas.

more people would grow herb gardens if given the thyme.

growing vegetables keeps a man on the straight and marrow.

cross a gardener with a fortune teller and they'll see
into the fuchsia.

some places charge the earth for compost.

broad beans should go on a diet.

one has to accept weeds, worts and all.

buying a new watering can is nothing to spout about.

*David's
book
of Nonsense*

Music & Musicians

classical composers enjoyed going late night Chopin.

an expensive drum kit is simply a status cymbal.

noisy drummers should beware of repercussions.

if you cannot master the guitar, don't fret.

honest violinists never fiddle their expenses.

incompetent composers needed a good Haydn.

too many overweight musicians on the internet
mean broad-band.

chamber music went to pot around the 1800's.

classical composers often led a Bizet life.

Our Health

they who have insomnia should not lose any sleep over it.

your audiologist always "looks forward to hearing from you".

eat whilst jumping over a rope, and you're skipping meals.

if men tend to get hernias, should it not rather be hisnias?

rude dermatologists really get under your skin.

choose an expensive chiropodist and you will foot the bill.

unhelpful chiropractors really get your back up.

for those who cannot give blood, it's all in vein.

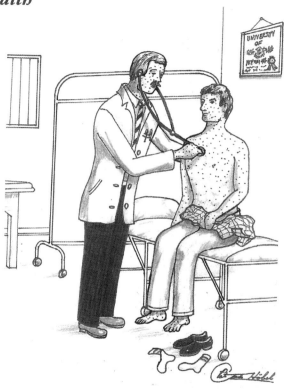

he who diagnoses measles makes a rash statement.

David's
of **Nonsense**
book

Technology

even keyboard designers can make a hash of things.

good I.T people are often recommended via word and mouse.

some flying insects navigate via gnat-nav.

frankly, hydropower construction workers do give a dam.

Norway invented the Lapland computer.

you may think you're computer literate but have you
ever read one ?

wind turbines are revolutionary.

at lunchtime, I.T specialists usually stop for a byte.

The Fishing Industry

in times of hardship, even lobster fishermen feel the pinch.

recent shortages of north sea flatfish saw sales flounder.

fish swim quicker when fitted with a turbotcharger.

a belligerent fisherman is soon put firmly in his plaice.

some sea creatures are shellfish and like to mussel in.

if fish owe you money, it's generally six-squid.

one can fish all day and not see a sole.

when a fish shop vacancy comes up they have to fillet fast.

David's
book
of Nonsense

History

*economical admirals such as Nelson often got 60 to
the galleon.*

incompetent medieval horsemen could be a real knightmare.

the Romans were generous and regularly donated to charioty.

*towns in American westerns always had a saloon,
never a hatchback.*

*medieval archers came from London settlements such
as Bow & Harrow.*

Wyatt Turp was a gunslinger who cleaned paint brushes.

the highwayman Dick Turnip was not dyslexic.

Central Americans invented the Rubik Cuba.

DIY

shoddy joinery is often a saw point.

a plasterer gets paid for services rendered.

they who mislay their ladder shall take the necessary steps to find it.

putting up shelving can be nerve racking.

electricity hertz!

wallpapering is ok once you get the hang of it.

replacing your roof fills the home with fun and rafter.

building a wall badly will leave you mortarfied.

David's book of Nonsense

Aviation & Space

Aviation

to design an aircraft, start with a blank piece of paper.

is there an airport in the world that is actually finished?

early aviators were Wright all along.

Space

when visiting an observatory one should planet first.

even astronauts need their own space sometimes.

saturn is superior and runs rings round other planets.

astronomers usually take a Sirius approach to their work.

Around the World

in Belgium, watering cans are known as Brussels spouts.

economical place Africa, you get many Niles to the gallon.

if your job is in Jeopardy, where exactly is that?

things happen at random, so where is random?

vodkaphone is not the Russian mobile network.

coco koala is a popular Australian drink.

the Scandinavian medical system is known as the National Elk Service.

Norwegians like their cars, especially Fiords.

Around the World

the International dateline is just a row of palm trees.

some roads on coffee plantations have filter lanes.

temples have to endure all weather come rain and shrine.

the heaviest place in Britain is the Isle of Weight.

boomerangs are making a comeback.

he who wears a jumper for 7 days shall have a week in Jersey.

some religions talk at cross purposes.

the tower of Pisa is currently going through lean times.

This is your opportunity to craft your own nonsense slogan, over the next pages you will find two cartoons that develop your literal style !

David's
of *book*
Nonsense

Reader's homework (i)

*this is where you get to make up your own
nonsense slogan to the sketch.*

Reader's homework (i)

_____

_____

_____

_____

_____

_____

_____

_____

answers page.

David's
book
of Nonsense

another chance to create your own nonsense slogan!

Reader's homework (ii)

_____

_____

_____

_____

_____

_____

_____

_____

answers page.

David's
of ***book***
Nonsense

David's
book
of
Nonsense